What is Informational Writing?

Charlotte Guillain

raintree
a Capstone company — publishers for children

Raintree is an imprint of Capstone Global Library Limited, a company incorporated in England and Wales having its registered office at 7 Pilgrim Street, London, EC4V 6LB – Registered company number: 6695582

www.raintree.co.uk
myorders@raintree.co.uk

Edited by Clare Lewis and Penny West
Designed by Philippa Jenkins and Tim Bond
Picture research by Gina Kammer
Originated by Capstone Global Library Ltd
Produced by Helen McCreath
Printed and bound by CTPS

ISBN 978 1 406 29684 6
19 18 17 16 15
10 9 8 7 6 5 4 3 2 1

British Library Cataloguing in Publication Data
A full catalogue record for this book is available from the British Library.

Acknowledgements
We would like to thank the following for permission to reproduce photographs:
Alamy: © Graham Franks, 5; Capstone Studio: Karon Dubke, 13, 18, 20, 21, 22, 23, 24, 27, 28; Dreamstime: © Elena Elisseeva, 7, © Konstantin Anisko, 29, © Serrnovik, 11, © Yvon52, 6; iStockphoto: mediaphotos, 9, 25; Shutterstock: Kinga, 4, Lisa F. Young, 26, MarclSchauer, 14, Milena Moiola, 15, Monkey Business Images, 10, Radu Bercan, 8

Disclaimer
All the internet addresses (URLs) given in this book were valid at the time of going to press. However, due to the dynamic nature of the internet, some addresses may have changed, or sites may have changed or ceased to exist since publication. While the author and publishers regret any inconvenience this may cause readers, no responsibility for any such changes can be accepted by either the author or the publishers.

Contents

Some words are shown in bold, **like this**. You can find out what they mean by looking in the glossary.

A world of non-fiction

When you go to school you are constantly learning new subjects. You learn about what happened in the past when you study history. You start to understand how the world works when you study science. You find out about different places in the world in geography and explore the work of famous artists, musicians and writers. Much of what you read at school is **non-fiction**. Non-fiction is any type of text that tells you about real-life facts and events.

You read and write non-fiction all the time at school.

The information on your food packaging is non-fiction.

However, non-fiction isn't just something you come across at school. You're reading non-fiction when you follow instructions to build or make something. When people read news articles in papers or on the internet, they are reading non-fiction. You're even reading non-fiction when you read the ingredients on the back of your cereal packet in the morning! This book is about **informational writing** – and this book *is* informational writing, too!

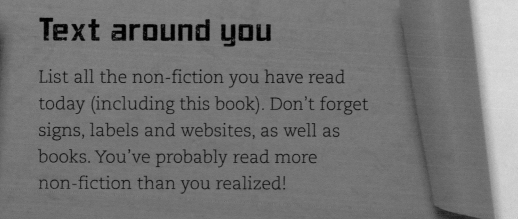

Text around you

List all the non-fiction you have read today (including this book). Don't forget signs, labels and websites, as well as books. You've probably read more non-fiction than you realized!

What is informational writing?

Informational writing answers questions that the reader might have on a **topic**. It provides details and explanations to help the reader start to understand the subject. This type of text describes processes and events clearly. When people write informational texts they need to think carefully about what the reader might already know about the subject. Sometimes the reader might know nothing about the topic before they read a text.

Text around you

The facts you find in information books might not always be true. People are learning new things about the world all the time. This means that information books that were published a long time ago may no longer be right. Your grandparents might have read books when they were your age that would have different information to the non-fiction you read!

Signposts give you information about where to go.

Informational writing is different to other types of **non-fiction**, such as instructional or persuasive writing. It doesn't try to change the reader's opinions. Informational writing is a piece of text that could be a page or a whole book, which gives the reader information on a specific subject. Informational writing could be a printed book, an ebook or a website.

Where can you find informational writing?

The main places you will find **informational writing** are your school and local library. The books in school libraries are useful because their writers wrote them for younger readers. Writers of information books also group the information so that it's clear.

Librarians order information books on the shelves in two ways. First, they look at the subject of the book and put it on a shelf with other books about that subject. Then the books within a subject are arranged in alphabetical order, based on the author's surname.

You can usually find the books you need quickly because of the way librarians organize the shelves.

Text around you

Informational text is also on websites. The internet is fantastic because you can find information very quickly. However, you need to take care that the information you find is true. Good websites for informational text include museum sites, news organizations' websites and online encyclopaedias.

Why do people read informational writing?

Readers need **informational writing** for many different reasons. Pupils use a range of information books when they're researching a project for homework. Other people read informational texts to get the information they need for a hobby or activity, for example, how to care for a new pet. Some informational writing gives you the facts you need to understand a subject or learn a new skill.

Reading informational text can open the door to many fun activities and hobbies.

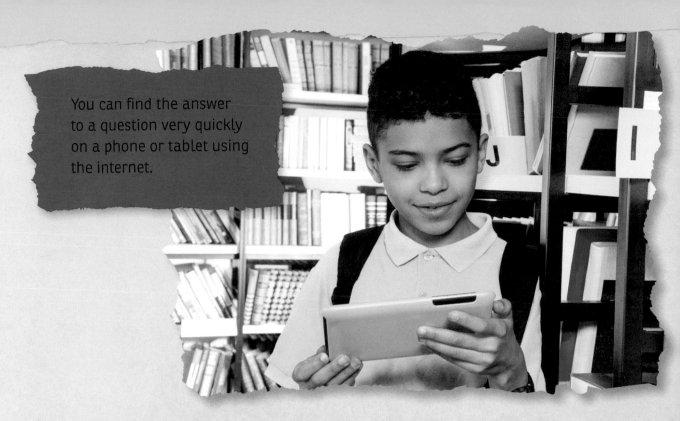

You can find the answer to a question very quickly on a phone or tablet using the internet.

Often people use information books as a quick reference to find out certain facts or details. You don't normally have to read an information book from the start to the finish. You can dip in and find the sections that interest you. People often search for information texts on the internet when they need a quick answer to a question.

Text around you

Not that long ago there was no internet. People had to go to a library or bookshop to find information books. Now, you are just as likely to use a tablet or computer to read informational writing.

What are the features of informational writing?

Printed informational texts have several features:

- The text in **informational writing** is usually divided up into sections. These are known as parts, chapters or double-page spreads.

- The different sections in an information book or informational text on the internet usually have **headings** and **sub-headings**. These help to break up the text and order the information clearly.

- Often the writers of informational texts ask questions in their headings. These questions are then answered by the text under the headings.

- Informational writing often includes short pieces of information, for example, in text boxes. These are quick facts that the reader can find without reading the entire book.

- Other information is presented in **bulleted lists** so it can be read and understood quickly.

What New Worlds Did the Vikings Explore?

The Vikings were forced to look for new lands to settle, because they were running out of good farmland at home. They were helped in this by changes in the climate. The weather became warmer than it had been in earlier centuries. This meant that the Vikings could explore new lands for a longer part of the year.

Iceland

By 870 ce the Vikings had moved farther west to Iceland. Even though farming was difficult in the cold, windy island, the settlements there grew rapidly. By 930 ce there were 30,000 people. A hundred years later, this figure had doubled to 60,000.

In Iceland, the Vikings established a **thing** to make and enforce laws. It became known as the Althing, and it still survives today as Iceland's national parliament.

Furs for nuts

Greenland's Viking settlers traded polar bear skins, walrus ivory, and furs for timber, tools, and special treats like raisins and nuts.

THEN...

Some experts call the Vikings the first oceanographers. Viking settlers used ocean currents to decide where to build towns and farms. In 874 ce, Ingólfur Arnarson threw wooden pillars overboard as he approached Iceland. He made his home where the wood landed (present-day Reykjavik, Iceland's capital). He knew that the ocean currents that guided the wood to land would also help ships find their way.

20

Greenland

In 982 ce the Viking Eric the Red set sail westward from Iceland. He saw a new land covered with ice. He called his discovery Greenland. It was colder than Iceland and it was not green, but he hoped that naming it Greenland would encourage others to join his settlement. The first settlers built dairy and sheep farms. Under Eric's leadership, Greenland's population reached 3,000.

This modern painting shows Eric the Red setting sail for Greenland with the crew of his Viking longship.

...NOW

Today, ships still use ocean currents to cut fuel costs. For example, a major shipping company in Japan tracks ocean currents. Then it guides its fleet of large oil carriers into the currents to save fuel.

21

You can see many typical features of informational writing on this spread.

Text tips!

In your own writing, try to break up long sections of text. It's much easier for the reader to take in information from short paragraphs with sub-headings.

Try to include bulleted lists and fact boxes. This also makes your writing more interesting.

gorillas. She uncovered many new facts about these gentle giants. She brought the gorillas to the attention of the world. Thanks to Fossey, people all over the globe came to know the gorillas she had named Digit, Peanuts, and Uncle Bert. And just like her, people came to care deeply about whether these animals lived or died.

Fossey was not afraid to make enemies to protect her gorillas. She waged war against those who tried to harm the animals. In the end, her **aggressive** methods led to her death. But Fossey's work did not die with her. Today people around the world still work to make sure that gorillas do not become **extinct**.

DID YOU KNOW?
- There are just two species of gorillas in the world: eastern gorillas and western gorillas. Mountain gorillas fall within the eastern gorilla group.
- Gorillas, chimps, orangutans, bonobos are **great apes**, humankind's closest living relatives.
- Male mountain gorillas can grow to be up to 485 pounds (220 kilograms) and 5 feet, 6 inches (168 centimeters) tall when standing upright.

5

Pictures in informational writing

Many information books include colourful photographs or artwork to illustrate the subject of the book. It would be hard to really learn about an unusual animal, such as the okapi, without seeing photographs of it!

Other images in informational texts can include diagrams. Diagrams often show how things work or help to explain something. They help the reader to understand the information much more quickly.

A description of an okapi gives you some information about the animal but a picture shows you what it looks like.

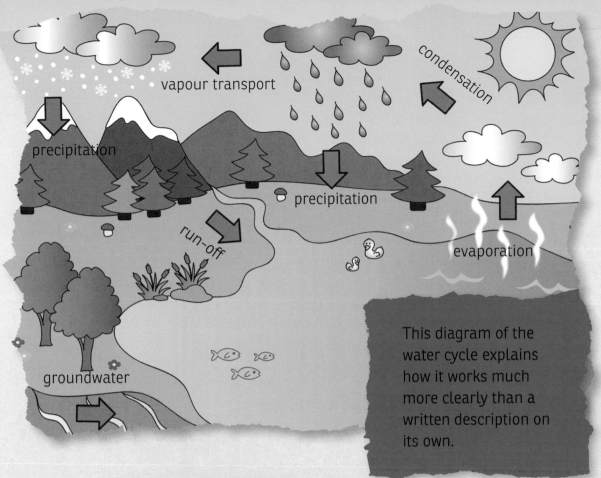

vapour transport

condensation

precipitation

precipitation

run-off

evaporation

groundwater

This diagram of the water cycle explains how it works much more clearly than a written description on its own.

You'll also find maps, timelines and **infographics** in many informational texts. Infographics are illustrations such as charts and graphs. Writers use infographics to show the reader information quickly.

Text tips!

If you include images in a piece of **informational writing,** add labels to say what the different parts of the picture show. For photos, write captions to add more information. Maps and diagrams usually need a **key** to explain what the different colours or symbols mean.

How to give information:
Writing up the results of a survey

Do a survey in your class and write up the results with a chart.

1. Decide what your survey is going to be about. You could find out your classmates' favourite sport to play.

2. Think of a clear question to ask your class members, for example "What is your favourite sport?"

3. Do your survey and keep a record of everyone's answers. You might want to write their answers in a table using **tally marks**.

What is your favourite sport?	
football	ⵚⵚ ⵚⵚ ‖
gymnastics	ⵚⵚ ‖‖
netball	ⵚⵚ ⵚⵚ ⵚⵚ ‖
swimming	ⵚⵚ ‖‖‖

4. When you have surveyed everyone, add up the tally marks. See how many people preferred each sport. Add up the total number of people you spoke to and keep a record of this, too.

5. Now write up the results of your survey. Start by writing what it was you wanted to find out and then explain how you went about finding the answers. Include what was the most popular choice of sport. Comment on whether any of the results surprised you.

6. Now produce your chart. Will it be a bar chart or a pie chart? Use different colours to represent each answer and include a **key**.

netball

football

swimming

gymnastics

7. Share your results with your classmates.

Signposts in informational writing

People who read **informational writing** often want to find certain information or facts. They might not want to read the entire text to find this. Signposts help them find the information they want. One signpost is the table of contents. It is always found at the start of an informational text. It shows the reader what the main sections are and their page numbers.

The table of contents tells you at a glance what information is in the book.

Contents

Some words are shown in **bold**, like this. You can find out what they mean by looking in the glossary.

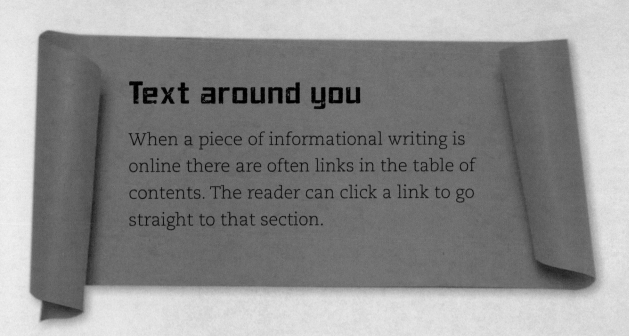

Text around you

When a piece of informational writing is online there are often links in the table of contents. The reader can click a link to go straight to that section.

There are also signposts at the end of informational writing. The **glossary** highlights words from the text that the reader may not have come across before and explains what they mean. The **index** is usually at the very end of the book. Here you'll find different **topics** covered by the text and listed in alphabetical order, along with page numbers. If, for example, you want to look up "signposts" in this book, go to the index and see what page numbers are listed after the word "signposts".

What sort of language is used in informational writing?

The purpose of **informational writing** is to explain or describe something to the reader. It usually starts with an **introduction**. This states what the rest of the text will be about.

Informational text usually finishes with a **conclusion**. The conclusion is a summary of what the book was about. The writer may ask questions in a conclusion to encourage the reader to find out more. He or she might answer questions that were asked in the introduction. The conclusion should round the text off neatly.

The introduction shows what areas the writing will explore.

Introducing Poland

What do you know about Poland? Do you have a friend whose family came from Poland? Do you know where Poland is or how big it is? Would you like to know more about this country's people, history, and geography?

A land of contrasts

Poland is in central Europe. The country covers 120,728 square miles (312,685 square kilometers), making it slightly smaller than the state of New Mexico. Its turbulent history stretches back over centuries. Neighboring countries have often invaded Polish lands.

Poland has many different regions, each with its own special character and traditions. Polish cities are a mix of old and new buildings, and the damage caused long ago by wars and foreign invasions can still be seen today. Visitors to Poland enjoy its beautiful landscapes, traditional **culture**, friendly people, and hearty food.

People on the move

Throughout history, Polish people have traveled around the world. Some have left hoping to find a better life in other countries. However, today many Poles are returning to Poland to share in its success in the 21st century. Read on to find out what makes Poland and its people so special.

MARIE CURIE (1867–1934)

Marie Curie is one of the world's most famous Poles. She left Poland to study in Paris when she was 24. In 1903, she won the **Nobel Prize** for physics with her husband Pierre Curie. They had discovered the **radioactive** elements polonium and radium. She was the first woman to win a Nobel Prize. She won it again in 1911 for her wo...

Can you find other examples of writing in the third person and present tense?

Feeding Time

Woof! Woof! It's dinner time and I'm hungry. I need food and water every day to keep me fit and healthy. You can feed me dry or wet dog food. Dry food is better for my teeth. You can buy this from the pet shop or supermarket.

14

Ruff's Top Meal-Time Tips

🐾 Adult dogs like me need two meals a day. Puppies need three to four smaller meals.

🐾 Some human foods, such as chocolate, raisins, and onions, are poisonous to dogs.

🐾 Make sure that I always have clean, fresh water to drink.

🐾 Don't feed me too many treats. They can make me overweight and unhealthy.

🐾 Sometimes give me a chewy bone to help clean my teeth.

15

The writer will often compare and contrast ideas in an information text to explain things. He or she presents facts truthfully and clearly. The writer doesn't usually focus on emotions or feelings.

Text around you

Informational writing is usually written in the **third person** and in **present tense**. This means the writer is describing the situation as it is now, for example, "Dogs need to be walked every day." However, an informational text about historical events would use the past tense, such as "People walked their dogs every day."

How to give information: Writing a mini book

Write a mini information book about a subject you're interested in.

1. Choose a subject. Pick something you know a lot about or one you find interesting.

2. Think of some questions that you think your book should answer. For example, in a book on elephants one question might be "What do elephants eat?"

3. Now you'll need to find the answers. Do some research at the library or online. Choose websites you can trust, such as big organizations and encyclopaedias.

4. Jot down your research notes. This will make it easier for you to write in your own words later.

5. Now plan your book. What will the structure be? Use your questions as the table of contents.

6. Write the book's **introduction**. Tell the reader what your book is about and why that subject is interesting.

7. Give each section a **heading** – the headings should be the questions you started with. Write the answer to each question in your own words.

8. Add photos, drawings and charts to illustrate the subject. Don't forget to include labels and captions.

9. Write your **conclusion**.

10. Add a **glossary** and **index** at the end of your book.

11. Make a cover and staple your book together. Share it with family and friends.

Thinking about the reader

Like all writers, authors of informational texts need to think carefully about their readers. How much does the reader already know about the subject? A book about crocodiles for very young children will explain that a crocodile is an animal with four legs and sharp teeth. However, a book about crocodiles for older readers will cover more complicated information, like how a crocodile manages to breathe under water. In books for older readers the writer can write much longer sentences and use more complicated language.

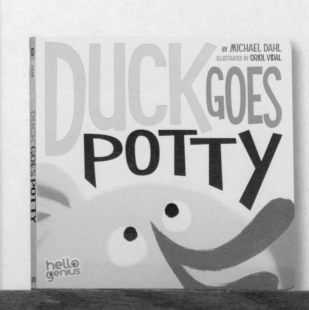

Good writers always keep their reader in mind as they write.

Writers also have to think about whether to use **formal** or **informal** language. **Informational writing** is usually more formal because the writer doesn't know who the reader will be and he or she is trying to explain a subject clearly. The writer needs to think of ways to make readers interested and hook them in so they carry on reading.

Text tips!

A good way to grab your reader's attention is to ask them questions at the beginning of your piece of writing. When you ask the reader a question, he or she will start to wonder what the answer is and hopefully will want to read on to find out!

How to give information:
Writing a guide to your school

Write a guide to your school for a new pupil who has just arrived from another country.

1. Plan your guide. Think of questions that a new pupil might have about your school.

2. How will you order your guide? Start it with an **introduction** and then decide in what order you will put the other information. Once you have a plan, write your table of contents, using your questions as the section **headings**.

3. Write each section of your guide under the headings. Can you add any **sub-headings**? Make sure you explain everything clearly for someone who has never been to a school like yours before.

4. Check you've included the most important details, such as the times that school starts and finishes, the names of teachers and the equipment a new pupil will need.

5. Check that your spelling and grammar are correct or you might confuse your reader!

6. Can you add any photos, maps or diagrams to help the new pupil find their way around?

7. It might be useful to include a **glossary** of school words in case the new pupil isn't familiar with school life in your country.

8. Show your guide to a friend and ask them if they think you've included all the important information.

The "Find out more" section

An information text is often a reader's first stop on a journey to find out more about a subject. Many writers include a "Find out more" section at the end of their book to help to point readers in the right direction. Usually this section suggests ways the reader can find more information in other books and websites. It can also include interesting places to visit.

Writers often also include a **bibliography** at the end of their **informational writing**. A bibliography tells the reader where the writer found the information they researched to write his or her book. The reader can look at the bibliography to find other texts on the subject to explore it in more depth.

Use the "Find out more" section of a book to learn even more about the subject.

grid reference figure made up of numbers and letters, or just numbers, that allows you to pinpoint a place on a map

key list of symbols and an explanation of what each one represents

latitude distance between the equator and a point north or south on Earth's surface. The distance is measured in degrees.

longitude distance on Earth's surface that is east or west of the prime meridian. The distance is measured in degrees.

natural feature something on Earth's surface that has been created by nature, for example, a mountain

Find Out More

There is a whole world of maps and mapping waiting to be discovered! Try looking at some other books and some web sites to get started.

Books

Henzel, Cynthia Kennedy. Reading Maps (On the Map). Edina, Minn.: ABDO, 2008.

Johnson, Jinny. Maps and Mapping (Inside Access). Boston: Kingfisher, 2007.

Torpie, Kate. Reading Maps (All Over the Map). New York: Crabtree, 2008.

Web sites

education.nationalgeographic.com/education/multimedia/interactive/maps-tools-adventure-island/kd/?ar_a=3
this interactive game to learn more about how symbols work

A book on the ocean might suggest museums or historical sites to visit to find out more.

Text tips!

When you are writing your own **non-fiction** text, always keep a record of the places where you found your information. Keep a list of the books you read and the websites you visited so you can find them again if you need to. Your readers can visit them too.

Glossary

bibliography list of books and websites used by an author

bulleted list list of items presented with bullet points

conclusion ending to a piece of writing

formal following the expected rules

glossary list of words with definitions (what the words mean)

heading words at the start of a section of writing that tell you what the section will be about

index list of words in a book with page numbers where you will find that word

infographic chart or graph that provides information

informal relaxed and not following all the rules

informational writing writing that increases the reader's knowledge or explains something clearly, such as a process or idea

introduction beginning of a piece of writing that explains what topic the writing will cover

key guide to what the different colours or symbols mean on a chart, graph or map

non-fiction writing about real-life facts

present tense writing that describes events that are happening now

sub-heading words that mark out a section of text within a larger section

tally mark mark used to keep count

third person when a writer talks about "her", "him" or "they"

topic a subject to talk about

Find out more

To learn more about how to gather, order and present information, take a look at the following books and websites. Use your findings and the "How to" topics in this book to test out your new informational writing skills!

Books

Evaluating Information (Information Literacy Skills), Beth A. Pulver (Heinemann Library, 2009)

Organizing and Using Information (Information Literacy Skills), Beth A. Pulver (Heinemann Library, 2009)

The Structure of Words: Understanding Roots and Smaller Parts of Words (Find Your Way with Words), Liz Miles (Raintree, 2014)

Websites

www.bbc.co.uk/nature
If you are looking for information about animals, the BBC Nature website is a great place to start.

www.britannica.com
The Encyclopedia Britannica online has information about most things you will want to research.

kids.nationalgeographic.com
You can find out lots about our world on the National Geographic Kids website.

www.nhm.ac.uk/kids-only/index.html
The Natural History Museum website includes plenty of information about the natural world.

www.sciencemuseum.org.uk/online_science.aspx
Find out about science on the Science Museum website.

Index